SO-ACT-296
HARRIS COUN...

J 590 Min
Minden, Cecilia
Push and pull
WITHDRAWN
$12.79
ocn916684780

ANIMAL OPPOSITES
PUSH AND PULL

by Cecilia Minden

Cherry Lake Publishing • Ann Arbor, Michigan

Published in the United States of America
by Cherry Lake Publishing
Ann Arbor, Michigan
www.cherrylakepublishing.com

Reading Adviser: Marla Conn, ReadAbility, Inc.

Photo Credits: © Anneka/Shutterstock Images, cover, 8; © Julie Vader/
Shutterstock Images, 4; © Svetlana Valoueva/Shutterstock Images, 6;
© smereka/Shutterstock Images, 10; © Jodie Nash/Shutterstock
Images, 12; © namatae/Shutterstock Images, 14; © puttsk/Shutterstock
Images, 16; © Kathy Kay/Shutterstock Images, 18; © M.M./Shutterstock
Images, 20; © Pictureguy/Shutterstock Images, 20; © DavidTB/
Shutterstock Images, 20; © SJ Allen/Shutterstock Images, 20;

Copyright ©2016 by Cherry Lake Publishing
All rights reserved. No part of this book may be reproduced or utilized in
any form or by any means without written permission from the publisher.

Library of Congress Cataloging-in-Publication Data
Minden, Cecilia, author.
 Push and pull / by Cecilia Minden.
    pages cm.—(Animal opposites)
 Audience: K to grade 3.
  ISBN 978-1-63470-474-8 (hardcover)—ISBN 978-1-63470-594-3 (pbk.)—
ISBN 978-1-63470-534-9 (pdf)—ISBN 978-1-63470-654-4 (ebook)
 1. Animals—Juvenile literature. 2. Concepts—Juvenile literature.
3. Vocabulary. I. Title.
 QL49.M6746 2016
 590—dc23
                                                     2015026049

Cherry Lake Publishing would like to acknowledge
the work of the Partnership for 21st Century Skills.
Please visit *www.p21.org* for more information.

Printed in the United States of America
Corporate Graphics

TABLE OF CONTENTS

Pets

A cat can push through a **flap** in the door.

What Do You See?

What color is the dog?

This dog is pulling on its **leash**.

Farm Animals

Baby goats are called kids. They push heads when they play.

What Do You See?

What is in the cart?

The horse lives on a farm.
It can pull a cart.

Zoo Animals

Kangaroos use their arms to push each other when they play.

What Do You See?

What is the monkey doing?

Monkeys can climb trees. They pull themselves up to get to the top.

Water Animals

The beaver pushes sticks together to make a home.

The **stork** has a long beak.
It can pull fish out of the water.

Which animals are pushing?

Which animals are pulling?

Find Out More

BOOK

Horáček, Petr. *Animal Opposites*. Somerville, MA: Candlewick Press, 2013.

WEB SITE

The Activity Idea Place—Opposites
www.123child.com/lessonplans/other/opposites.php
Play some games to learn even more opposites.

Glossary

flap (FLAP) a part that hangs loose and on the side of something

kangaroos (kang-guh-ROOS) Australian animals with short front legs and long back legs used for jumping

leash (LEESH) a strap or chain that you use to hold and control an animal

stork (STORK) a large bird with thin legs, a long neck, and a straight bill

Home and School Connection

Use this list of words from the book to help your child become a better reader. Word games and writing activities can help beginning readers reinforce literacy skills.

animals	goats	push
arms	heads	pushing
baby	home	sticks
beak	horse	stork
beaver	kangaroo	their
called	kids	themselves
cart	leash	they
climb	lives	through
color	monkeys	together
doing	other	trees
door	out	water
each	pets	what
farm	play	when
fish	pull	which
flap	pulling	zoo

Harris County Public Library
Houston, Texas

Index

About the Author

Cecilia Minden, PhD, is a former classroom teacher and university professor. She now enjoys working as an educational consultant and writer for school and library publications. She has written more than 150 books for children. Cecilia lives in and out, up and down, and fast and slow in McKinney, Texas.